The
GREATEST
MOTIVATIONAL
TOOL

The Greatest Motivational Tool
Discover the Secret to Maximizing Performance
in the 21st Century

Copyright © 2019 by Rod Olson

ISBN: 9781795000574

To learn more about Rod Olson,
visit **RodOlson.org**

DEDICATION

This book is dedicated to all the coaches and leaders who recognize that people are the competitive separator. Thank you for being deliberate about caring for your people and making time for them. I also want to dedicate this book to the special forces operators of the United States military who tirelessly serve our country, and to the numerous SEALs I've been fortunate to work with over the years. You have impacted my life and family in more ways than you will ever know.

Lastly, this is for Keene, Keli, Joe, Mark and Joey. You made a difference and we miss you.

FOREWORD
BY JON GORDON

When I talk about the power of positive leadership, many at first think I'm just going to talk about having a positive mindset. While that's a big part of it to help us overcome our challenges, positive leadership is much more than a positive state of mind that makes us think and feel better. It's also a positive state of action that makes the people around us better.

I met Rod Olson several years ago at a spring training staff meeting when I was speaking to the Pittsburgh Pirates players and coaches. Rod was sharing coaching and leadership tips with all the coaches in the room, and I later learned Rod has been working with the Pirates organization for years helping develop their coaches and leaders. Rod and I became friends immediately and I kept in touch with him and his work. When I received his newsletter discussing the power of one-on-one meetings, I emailed him and told him how he needed to put his thoughts and practices into a leadership fable, much like he did previously in his excellent book,

The Legacy Builder. I'm thankful he did because I know you will benefit from this book.

Positive leadership is all about building great relationships with the people you lead to build great teams that can accomplish something amazing together. Over the years, I have discovered and shared with countless leaders that the best way to do this is through one-on-one meetings with the people you lead. After all, you can't lead and motivate someone if you don't know what motivates them. You have to get to know someone in order to lead them and help them be their best so they can give their best to the team and organization.

This is why I absolutely love this book. Rod Olson does a masterful job sharing the importance and power of one-on-one meetings while giving us the practical tools to make them effective and impactful. I believe reading this book will transform the way you lead and by following his simple step-by-step approach, you will transform your team and people in the process.

Rod shows us that the greatest way to motivate is not through big speeches, bold strategy meetings or loud screaming sessions with your team. The greatest way to motivate is through one-on-one meetings that enhance communication, develop connection and strengthen commitment one team member at a time.

The truth is if you don't have time for one-on-one meetings with your team, you don't have time to be a great leader. The key is to make time. Make it a priority. Read this book, which will take less than a few hours, create your plan and then make it a daily practice at work and home. You'll be glad you did.

-Jon Gordon

CONTENTS

Chapter 1
Your Numbers Are Down

"So you'll send me the paperwork?"

"Absolutely!" Peter grinned, a sense of satisfaction filling his chest. Nothing felt better than getting the signature on a new contract. *ABC. Always Be Closing.* He lived for the deal. This one had taken all his skills of persuasion during numerous phone calls, two video conferences, and four lunches, just like this one. But it was done.

His phone, tucked beneath the edge of his plate, buzzed quietly on the linen tablecloth. Peter glanced down. Gabrielle, his assistant. It could wait.

Peter pushed back the chair and put out his hand as he got up. "I'll have them on your desk by Monday morning, if not before."

The client stood and shook his hand. "I look forward to doing business with you."

Peter strode back to his car, unable to stop smiling. Life was good. Work was better. This contract would mean they'd start the new quarter off with a huge head start. The latest quarter had ended with the best margins he'd seen since taking over the CEO position three years ago. They had hired him to improve profits and industry position, and he'd done both.

He opened his car, then paused a moment to let some of the heat out. He slipped off his suit coat and tossed it in the passenger seat, then got behind the wheel. His phone buzzed. He pulled it from his pocket, then dropped it on top of the coat as he started the car. His assistant again. What can she want? Gabrielle knew he was at lunch with the client.

Hot air blasted from the vents. He waited for the Bluetooth to kick in before calling her. "What's so urgent?"

Gabrielle didn't waste time. "The board chair called. They're having a called meeting of the board of directors tomorrow at four. He wants you to confirm before EOB today."

Peter frowned. "The whole board? What's it about?"

"He wouldn't say. Just wants your confirmation that you'll be there."

"No idea why it's so late in the day? On a Friday?"

This time she hesitated. "Apparently, some of the directors are only flying in for the meeting. They couldn't get here any earlier."

That made sense. One of the directors lived in Anchorage. "Okay. Go ahead and send him a confirmation. Do I have anything scheduled?"

"Just a follow-up call if today's lunch had not gone well. Did it?"

"Perfect. It's done! We just need to send the contract on Monday."

"I'll pull out what we've drafted so far and start polishing it. Oh, and you had planned to leave early tomorrow."

"Oh, that's right. Aaron starts basketball camp Saturday. I'd wanted to shoot some hoops with him. Maybe give him some pointers."

"Hope he won't be too disappointed."

Peter hesitated. Gabrielle didn't usually make such personal comments. Then Peter remembered that she had a son about twelve, Aaron's age. She probably understood, although Gabrielle never talked about her family at all. He cleared his throat. "Aaron didn't know. I wanted it to be a surprise."

"Ah. Are you coming back to the office?"

Why would he not . . . Peter glanced at the dashboard clock. Three-thirty already. "Wow! I didn't realize it was so late. But yeah, I'm headed that way. Can you print all the end-of-quarter reports from the team, including mine, and leave them on my desk?"

"No problem."

Peter ended the call, fastened his seat belt and pulled out of the lot. His stomach tightened as he thought about the board meeting. Why in the world would they need to call a board meeting now? The quarter had just ended, so they'd just been in the building less than a month ago. Interim meetings, if needed, were held by video conferencing. What would be so dire that they'd need to get them all in-house again?

His thoughts churned all the way back to the office, playing out one scenario after another about why the board would need to meet. Peter breezed into his office just before four. As requested, six quarterly reports were stacked on his desk, each in their own folders and marked clearly. A seventh folder held the current version of the client's contract, along with Gabrielle's questions and suggested corrections. Everything was on the server, but she knew he liked to review hard copy too.

He paused. Gabrielle did great work. He'd only been with the company for three years, and Gabrielle had trained him as to the inner workings of the organization. She "knew where the bodies were buried," so to speak. Her efficient and professional work certainly kept him on track. Maybe in all this, he could decipher what was going through his chairman's head.

Gabrielle asked if he needed anything else, and Peter shook his head. "I just want to spend some time with the numbers. See if I can figure out what's up. You can leave early, if you want to."

She nodded but gestured with her pen toward his own quarterly report. On the top was a sticky note with the chairman's personal cell number.

Peter snatched it up and saluted Gabrielle. "Thank you."

She nodded and left, and Peter sank into his chair. "Can't hurt to just ask." He punched in the number.

No answer. As the chairman's voicemail kicked in, Peter took a deep breath. "Joe, I got the message about tomorrow's meeting. Do I need to prepare anything special? Bring any reports that you might not have seen? The last quarter's numbers were fantastic! I thought everyone would be happy with the dividends. We certainly were around here. Call me."

Peter hung up, dropped his cell on his desk and walked to the window. Only thirty-eight stories up, but his office had an unobstructed view of the city. He liked it here.

No. He loved it here. One of the best job fits of his career. It hit all his sweet spots and matched his skill sets like nothing else he'd done. The first year of his contract, the company had increased profits by almost 10 percent. The next year, more than 20 percent. This year, they were on track to a major increase again, and they'd only finished the third quarter. His contract was up at the end of the fiscal year, but he was sure—

Peter's thoughts stopped. His contract. That had to be it. Joe had told him the board would let him know well before the end of the fiscal year whether his contract would be renewed. A smile spread over his face. Contract renewal.

Maybe even a raise. The whole board would have to sign off on an increase.

His phone buzzed on his desk, and Peter grabbed it up. A text from Joe: *No need to prepare. Just be there.*

Bingo.

"Ha! Peter, dude, you are worrying over nothing."

He dropped back into his chair and pulled the new client contract proposal closer. They might even get this out by tomorrow.

* * * *

The contract did, in fact, head out by messenger shortly before noon. Peter ate a quick lunch, then spent the afternoon going over all the reports. Just in case, he thought, if they have any questions about the numbers.

Peter stood, relaxed and ready, outside the boardroom at 3:55pm. Precisely at four, Joe's assistant opened the door. Peter stepped in and took a deep, steadying breath. The boardroom smelled like furniture polish and coffee, and he smiled as he faced the five men and four women seated at one end of the oblong table. The chair at the head of the table was empty, and Joe, sitting to the left of it, motioned for Peter to sit there. "Good afternoon, Peter."

"Good afternoon." Peter nodded at the directors. Each of them had a tablet open in front of them, and Joe slid one toward Peter. He centered it in front of him and stared at the screen. It was his quarterly report.

Joe cleared his throat. "We want to start by telling you that we are pleased with this quarter's numbers, as we have been the last two years. You've taken your charge to turn things around seriously, and we appreciate that. We have no quarrel with your industry performance."

Peter heard the unspoken "but" in that sentence and sat quite still, waiting. Joe clicked a few keys on his tablet, and all the screens changed simultaneously. Obviously, all networked together and under Joe's control. The new screen showed the cover page of a performance report. Peter's name was centered on the screen.

Joe addressed the board. "What's on your screens now is the white paper that was sent to you this week, which you should have had a chance to review, and which has precipitated today's decision."

Peter's stomach tightened. This did not sound like the beginning of a commendation.

Joe turned to Peter. His tone lowered and his voice was gentle but firm. "Peter, an issue has come up that has to be addressed." He began scrolling through the report. Your sales numbers are tremendous. What you've done for the company at large is to be praised. But there are other numbers that have to be taken into consideration." He stopped the report on a page that Peter recognized immediately—his employee engagement scores and likeability scores from the past quarter. He'd remembered seeing them previously but hadn't given them a second thought.

Peter placed his palms flat on the table, on either side of the tablet. The same scores had been low last year, and Joe had mentioned them, urging Peter to bring them up. But he was not here to be liked. He'd not been hired to be a cheerleader. His responsibility was to increase sales, not play scout leader. He started to speak, but Joe put up a hand.

"This is not to devalue what you have achieved."

Peter couldn't hold back. "What I've achieved has been record profitability. Productivity and profitability. That's why you hired me. I'm not a nursemaid. These people are adults. And they appreciate the fact that their bonuses will be higher this year than they have been since 1984."

Joe stiffened. "So it's too bad you're still leading like it's 1984."

Peter stared at him. "What?"

Joe leaned forward in his chair. "The era of Blockbuster Video and Kodak is over. This is the twenty-first century. You have to start leading like it. We need our leaders—especially our CEO—not only to produce but to also have great relationships with the staff and employees.

Every employee needs to feel cared about and valued, so we can retain our talented people and also so that we can attract the most gifted and talented people."

Heat rose in Peter's chest and face. "I didn't come here to be a people pleaser. I came to turn things around."

Joe hesitated, and several of the directors shifted in their chairs. "And you have. Unfortunately, you've alienated your team and most of the company in the process. I tried to tell you about this last quarter. Apparently, you didn't listen."

Peter nodded. "What do you want?"

Joe looked at the other directors, as if for confirmation. Two of them nodded. So did Joe as he turned to face Peter directly.

"We have decided to put you on a development plan. This plan will be incremental, as we will be asking your executive team and stakeholders for evidence of your growth in the area of employee engagement, and this will be done at the end of each of the next three quarters. We know this won't happen overnight, so this plan will be implemented immediately and we will do a comprehensive review of your progress at the completion of the fourth quarter of next year." Peter was dying inside... *a development plan for me, the CEO?* "You will have till the end of the fourth quarter of next year to bring up your employee engagement and likeability scores. If not, your contract will not be renewed."

Peter couldn't believe it. "You'll fire me because people don't like me."

"Your contract won't be renewed because your leadership skills are antiquated and twenty-five years behind the times. You will no longer represent the aims and goals of this organization." Joe closed his tablet. "I'll email you a copy of this report and development plan so you can see what went into it. The employee surveys will be done the last week of each quarter over the upcoming year. Again, you'll have until the end of the fourth quarter to make needed changes, but we suggest you start today."

Peter stood slowly, looked at each of the directors, then left the room. He held his temper as he left, but by the time he reached the elevator, he felt claustrophobic, as if he were choking. Fortunately, Gabrielle had already left by the time he reached his office. Peter slammed the door, jerked off his tie, and slung his coat across the room. With a bellow of anger, he cleared his desk with one swipe, sending everything flying, even the pictures of his wife and kids.

Peter stalked to the window, hitting it once with his fist. The glass bowed slightly, and the resulting boom echoed around the room.

What was he supposed to do? Bow and scrape to every whim of his people. Pamper them? Buy them gifts? He was kind to them, wasn't he? Usually?

"What do you want from me?"

Only silence answered his bellow, and he stared out at the city. The view that had brought him joy yesterday now made him feel out of depth. And old.

Peter rubbed his arm. Hitting the window had actually hurt. "Dude, that was stupid." He returned to his desk and dropped into his chair, his thoughts bouncing uncontrollably. Since he'd entered business at twenty-four, his career had been on an upward trajectory. No sidesteps. No major failures. Now...he'd be derailed because people didn't *like* him?

Worse than that, he didn't even know where to start, how to change.

"How can no one like me? I'm a good guy! I even have an open door policy for my team!"

Peter looked at his closed door. His exec team. That's the problem.

Peter got up, opened the door, and picked up his laptop from the floor. He opened it, checked email, and downloaded the promised report and development plan, vile thing that it was. He snarled as he read through it carefully. He opened a blank Word document and started making notes along the way, the pro and cons, complaints, all the up-and-down scores on the surveys.

He made a list of his executive team and made notes about all he knew about each one, things that related to work and those that didn't. The times they had come to him with a problem or a question about...anything. The lists were shorter than he expected, and he realized that almost none of them had actually made use of his "open door policy." Even requests for time off came via email.

Profits were up...but so were turnovers, even on his own team. Company-wide, resignations had increased by 30 percent since he'd taken charge. Two members of his executive team—two out of six!—had resigned. They'd cited family problems, but now, Peter had to wonder. He kept digging until his fury had abated and a slow dread settled over him.

"Maybe it is me." He leaned back in his chair, realizing that his back was stiff and sore. So was his arm. He glanced at the window again, shaking his head. He'd done dumb stuff before, but that was classic. It was dark outside, and his eyes felt dry. "What time is it?" Peter looked around for his phone. Still on the floor with the rest of the stuff from his desk.

He stood, stretched, and picked it up, shocked. It was almost six in the morning! His wife Mary had texted eight times, stopping with one around 11pm that read: *I'm going to bed. I can't believe you're still working. See you in the morning.*

He didn't dare call her now. Or should he? Peter sighed, but the question was answered when the phone rang in his hand. Great, he thought as he answered it. Trouble on both fronts.

CHAPTER 2
The Home Front

Peter watched the garage door slide shut behind his Jeep, well aware that locked inside the High Altitude edition of his Jeep Wrangler was probably the safest place on the planet for him at the moment. He dreaded going inside the house. Mary's angry words of hurt and doubt had blistered him, and Peter was grateful he had still been at the office. He'd texted her a picture of the sunrise from his office, one that included a view of the mess on his desk.

Not that he thought that would calm her down much. Peter took a deep breath and got out. Time to face the music.

The starkly silent kitchen smelled of bacon and eggs. Mary stood at the stove, slowly stirring a skillet of scrambled eggs. Sara sat at the bar, texting furiously. His 14-year-old daughter shot him one furious glance, then went back to texting. Aaron, age 12, hunched over the kitchen table, his thumbs dancing over his phone, probably in some kind of game. The wires from his earbuds danced with each movement. He did not look up.

Mary dished up eggs on two plates already holding toast and bacon. She sat them in front of the kids. "Phones down." They obeyed, digging into their breakfast. Mary finally turned to face him, leaning against the counter. "Do you want any breakfast?"

Peter shook his head. "I'm sorry."

Sara grabbed her plate and phone. "That's right. You're always sorry, Dad. But you never do anything about it!" She stalked out of the room.

Aaron stood up and picked up his plate. He shrugged and followed his sister down the hall.

Mary crossed her arms. "I'm waiting. What's the excuse this time?"

Peter draped his coat across one of the barstools. "The board had a called meeting late yesterday afternoon. It did not go well."

Mary scowled. "You said the numbers were good this quarter. Profits are up."

"They are. But they want more. My employee engagement and likeability scores have dropped. Bottomed out, more like it."

"So you behave at work the way you do around here."

Peter's chest tightened in pain. Wow. He blinked at his wife, not believing her words.

Mary must have seen the hurt in his face. She let out a long breath and dropped her arms to her side. "You are not making this easy, Peter. We matter too."

"Of course you do! It's just that . . ." His voice trailed off.

"It's just that . . . what?" Mary asked.

"I don't know what to do. I've got four quarters to get the scores up or they won't renew my contract."

"They'll fire you?"

Peter nodded. Mary closed her eyes a moment and turned her face to the ceiling, as if saying a prayer. When she spoke again, her voice was soft but firm. "Then you'd better figure it out. And quick." She turned and made sure the stove was off and moved the pans to the counter.

"And when you figure it out, you'd better put it to work here at home as well.

Things are starting come apart, although I don't suspect you've noticed. I can't do this alone, Peter. We have to get it together."

Without warning, Mary strode to the hallway and uncharacteristically shouted. "Sara! Get back in here. Time to leave. And bring your plate!"

Mary focused on Peter again. "Sara has volleyball practice. Did you remember that you have to drive Aaron to basketball camp this morning?"

Peter straightened. "Of course, I did."

Mary sniffed. "Right." She turned back to the hallway. "Sara! Come on! We're late!"

"I'll change. We'll get there on time."

His wife stepped closer. She bit her lower lip, then whispered, "Your son hasn't said a word in three days. Not to me. Not to Sara. You need to start paying attention, Peter.

You're losing grip on more than just your job. Are you hearing me?"

Peter nodded, a wave of sadness, of defeat, settling over him. "I hear you."

Sara strode through the kitchen, paused to put her plate in the dishwasher, then stalked out the garage door, slamming it behind her. Mary nodded, picked up her purse and followed.

Peter headed down the hallway, pausing at Aaron's door. Stickers from role-playing games, rock bands, and superhero movies clustered around a large MUGGLES KEEP OUT sign. Peter knocked, then pushed open the door. A mound of clothes partially blocked the door. The empty breakfast plate perched precariously on the edge of a desk cluttered with game paraphernalia and comics. Aaron lay on his bed, staring up at his phone, his fingers still working furiously over the screen.

"Hey, buddy."

Aaron cut his eyes toward his dad, then went back to playing.

Right. "I'm going to change, then we'll head to basketball camp. Be ready in five. OK?"

One nod.

Peter closed the door, his sadness becoming desperation. He had to find a way to fix this. All of it.

CHAPTER 3
Getting Coached Up

Peter drove in silence, trying to ignore the weariness that had started to sink into his bones. The adrenaline and stress of the all-nighter—and the confrontation with Mary—had drained away, leaving him exhausted.

Aaron leaned hard against the passenger door, his shoulders hunched and his earbuds in, that universal teenage signal of "leave me alone." And, for now, Peter would. For now.

The drive to the university, host of the basketball camp, was a familiar one. Peter and Mary's alma mater, the university had been a part of their entire adult lives. They'd both been involved since graduation as boosters with the athletic department, and Mary had served on several alumni committees. This was Aaron's second year at their summer basketball camp, and Peter had become friends with the head coach of the program, a man everyone called Coach O.

Aaron finally abandoned his phone, tucking it into his backpack, as Coach O gave instructions and sent the boys to ball handling drills. Peter sat about halfway up the first tier of bleachers, watching, his mind drifting aimlessly over the past few days. He was too tired to focus.

Coach O had greeted Peter when they'd first arrived, and now Peter realized the coach kept glancing at him. Finally, Coach made his way up the bleachers and sat down next to him.

"Hey, Peter, how are you?"

Peter shrugged. "Fine."

Coach looked him up and down. "Fine? Dude, you look as if you haven't slept in a month. What's going on?" Peter stared at his hands a moment, and Coach lowered his voice. "Work? Home?"

"Work," Peter said finally. He shrugged. "Maybe both. One into the other. We had a board meeting yesterday, and it went seriously south. I wound up staying at the office all night, which didn't exactly sit well with Mary."

Coach O held up a hand. "Hang on a minute, brother." He stood and motioned at one of his assistants.

"I'm supposed to run the next shooting drill; can you please take over for about 30 minutes? I need to take care of something." The assistant nodded and stepped in to change out one of the drills. Coach touched Peter on the shoulder. "I have a lot of flexibility during these youth camps. Let's go to my office. I want to hear all the details."

Peter stood and followed Coach out of the gym and down one of the corridors of the athletic center. Coach unlocked the door and ushered Peter into a room filled with sports memorabilia, posters, and trophies. A room that echoed the successes Coach had had over the years.

They both sat in chairs front of the desk, and Coach turned his chair to face Peter directly. "OK, Peter. Tell me what happened at the board meeting, from the beginning."

Peter started with the phone call from his assistant Gabrielle, his own arrogance about how well the company had performed under his leadership, and repeated Joe's comment about his "leading like it was 1984."

At which point, Coach O laughed. A full-blown belly laugh that bounced off the walls.

Peter stopped, staring at him. "What the—? I thought you were my friend!"

Coach O's laughed eased off, but he still grinned, his eyes bright with amusement. "Oh, my brother. I am not laughing at you. I'm laughing at the situation. Because I've lived through that exact conversation."

"You?" Peter gestured around the room. "You're one of the most successful men I know."

Coach leaned forward. "But I wasn't five years ago. Oh, we'd won a lot of games, a championship, had gone to the playoffs, all the outward trappings, but no one really liked me. Not my assistants, not even the janitor who cleans these offices. And the players and students didn't feel cared about. It got so bad that the athletic director called me in, told me I had to make a change . . . or *she* would have to make a change. She gave me one semester and a summer to make it happen."

Peter glanced around the room. "Yet here it is five years later and you're doing great."

"Yep."

"So what did you do? How did you change? I am at a complete loss. I don't even know where to start. How did you accomplish this?"

Coach shook his head.

"My athletic director told me my approach was not going to work long-term in today's world. She told me that if I planned to maximize the potential of my staff and players, they need to feel cared about by me and valued, or they'd find another program."

"That's exactly what the board said to me."

"You see, my athletic director was telling me what I really needed to hear about my leadership style, not just what I wanted to hear. She wasn't going to give me kudos just for winning games. She wanted me to build more than just a program. She wanted me to build a culture—which meant engaging people in a way that made them want to be process driven, take ownership and to stay with it. I was a transactional leader, which means mainly results driven. I wasn't a mean person; I just wasn't a *people first* person."

He paused. "Peter, I know it's hard. Believe me. But perhaps your board just did you a favor. They explained what you needed to hear."

"I'm definitely not a people pleaser." Peter let out a long breath. "To be honest, I'm not sure I can be."

Coach shook his head. "Don't get me wrong. This isn't about being a people pleaser. This is about truly connecting with the people you lead at a healthy and proper personal level. People today must feel safe, secure, and significant. All of us—employees, players, leaders, everyone—we are starving for authentic relationships with the people around us, the people we work and play with every day. The relationship between boss and employees is particularly vital. Online and digital relationships and friendships are fine, but we are humans and healthy, real relationships are as vital to us today as oxygen."

Coach O stood and sat on one corner of the desk. "Peter, my 'Why'—my reason or purpose for being a coach and a leader—used to be to win games, head for the playoffs and win a national title. I never got involved with others on a personal level. I would only meet with my staff or players in one-on-one meetings once a year for year-end evaluations—or what was becoming more frequent—exit interviews.

"Now my 'Why' is to help others reach their dreams and goals. What do they want to achieve? Now I meet with everyone on a monthly basis. It's a small thing, but you wouldn't believe the changes it's made. Everyone is performing at much higher levels, and team cohesion and synergy have gone through the roof."

He looked at Peter closely. "But you have to be present with all interactions.

You can't 'mail in' the one-on-one meetings. You just can't go through the motions. People can spot a selfish inauthentic leader from a mile away in today's world.

You must be intentional about scheduling time for them, authentically care about them, and you must have a systematic process that draws out what people want and how you can help them reach their potential and dreams. Remember, if you aren't valuing your people, you are devaluing them."

"So how did you learn all this? Where did you start?"

Coach O looked at his watch. "That's a much longer conversation. Why don't we meet for coffee Monday morning, and we can go through the whole drill? You in?"

Peter stood. "I'm all in. Although I do feel like I've just been shoved into the deep end of the swimming pool."

Coach laughed and clapped Peter on the back. "My brother, you ain't seen nothing yet!"

CHAPTER 4
Coffee with Coach O

The rest of the weekend, Peter tried to decompress, rest, and engage his family, experiencing only moderate success with all three. Sara mostly snapped at him, and Aaron only emerged from his room for meals. Mary tried to be open to conversation, but a distance had developed between her and Peter, and every attempt at a discussion fell flat.

Peter didn't blame Mary—or the kids. The more he thought about his work life over the past two years, the more he realized he'd been building walls between himself and almost everyone in his life. By the time Monday morning rolled around, Peter was more than ready to hear what Coach had to say.

The coffee shop where they met was a local place catering mostly to commuters and university students. At 8:30, most of the commuters had passed through and the college kids were either in class or still in bed. When Peter arrived, Coach O greeted him with a wave from a far corner where two comfy chairs waited. Peter got a large coffee and joined him.

Peter jumped right in. "Coach, you have to tell me what happened when the athletic director confronted you."

Coach O waited until Peter got settled. "Well, I was stunned, of course. Here I was, thinking I was doing just what they wanted, only to find out they needed something entirely different from me. And they had assumed I knew that!"

Peter set his coffee aside and took a notepad and pen from his briefcase. "I know. I think that was the hardest to hear. We definitely aren't on the same page, and I don't think either the board or I realized it until those scores came out."

Coach checked his watch. "How much time do you have?"

"I had my assistant block the whole morning. I really appreciate you taking the time to help me and coach me up on how to properly execute these one-on-one meetings."

Coach O nodded his head, chuckling.

Peter scowled. "Why is that funny?"

"Because you hit on the first thing to remember. You used the word 'execute.' This process—these meetings—aren't a business objective to execute.

If you keep thinking this is about business, you'll stay stuck in the same place. This is about dealing with people, and people will sense if your meetings with them are just another thing for you to check off your to-do list.

As I said before, people today are very perceptive and they will be able to tell if you authentically care about them and want to genuinely help them or if you are meeting with them to save your job and raise your engagement scores."

Peter stared at his blank note pad a moment, then wrote across the top "Not about business." He looked up again. "OK. So . . . what did you do?"

"I decided to go back to the basics. When you start learning to be a coach, who do you learn from?"

Peter scowled. "Other coaches."

"Exactly. So I talked to some other coaches, and I hired the best coach consultant I could find."

Peter leaned back in his chair. "Wait, bro. You're one of the best coaches in the country. *You* hired a coaching consultant?"

"Yeah, I did. I found someone who used to be a college coach himself, and he now helps coaches, college and professional, as well as business executives, be the best that they can be, both at work and at home. I hired him, and he taught me how to care about my people... authentically."

"So what did he teach you? What *could* he teach you?"

"Hold that thought." Coach O pulled a sheet of paper out of his notebook. "Before I get into that part, I want to show you this. The consultant I hired also does a monthly newsletter and a recent one featured an article that goes through what he had me do. The article covered a study that the *Harvard Business Review* has done, pointing out that the yearly review is becoming obsolete. It comes far too late in the process and lacks the immediate feedback that people are coming to expect in the 21st century. And many of the reviews are now automated. People don't even have to be in the same office when it happens. The supervisors do their part on the computer, then the employee completes. Sometimes they meet after, but they aren't required to do so."

Peter nodded. "Yeah, that's the way they're done at our company."

Coach shook his head. "Peter, that's not what employees really want. They don't want to learn a new program. They want interaction. They want coaching and help when they need it, and they don't want to wait until the end of the year for their feedback. By the time the end of the year—or their hiring anniversary—rolls around, it's too late to make any adjustments and offer help."

Coach pointed at the newsletter. "And my coach told me essentially the same thing. He taught me that I need to scrap my yearly evals and do quarterly evals. He also pointed out that in between the evaluations, I needed to do one-on-one meetings monthly with my staff. He showed me how to set them up, do them, and—"

Peter interrupted. "One-on-one meetings? With the whole staff? How do you have time to do that?"

"He told me that I didn't have time *not* to. If I didn't, I'd find myself doing exit interviews instead." Coach shifted in his chair to lean closer to Peter.

"Like I said yesterday, in the 21st century, management is more about getting to know your people than being a taskmaster. It's all about relationships, developing your people, and making them feel cared about.

It's about authenticity and genuine compassion."

Peter scribbled down "relationships, authenticity, and compassion." He took a deep breath. "I don't know if I'm up to this. Maybe I am too mired in the past."

Coach grinned. "No, you're not. It's not rocket science; it just takes a little getting used to, a few adjustments in your approach. Remember, you learned your style of management in the first place."

"Yeah, but I was a lot younger then."

Coach laughed and tapped the newsletter. "Look. Let's go over these points. Let's start with what most people complain about these days."

The Top Two Complaints from 21st-Century Players and Employees

1. "I just don't feel like they [their coach or boss] care about me as a person."
2. "I wish they would give me clearer expectations. It seems like they always wait until the end of the quarter or season to tell me how I was not performing the way they wanted me to."

The Top Two Complaints from 21st-Century Execs and Coaches

1. "We couldn't have been clearer in our expectations. Why aren't they

performing at the level we need them to?"

2. "We have parties; we do team building activities; yet we still have people and teams underperforming and complaining that they don't feel engaged and cared about. I want to know; how can we get in front of this?"

Peter stared at the newsletter. "That is *exactly* what I hear and probably exactly what we say as leaders."

Coach O went on, "It's all about communication. Everyone always says you can't overcommunicate your mission, vision, and values enough. Well, you can't overcommunicate your expectations enough either, especially with the people you lead. That includes our own children.

If people feel like they are valued and that you are growing them both professionally and personally, they will rarely leave for another job or team.

Or stay away from you and your wife to the point that the family comes apart."

Peter shifted uncomfortably. "It's as if you've been looking over my shoulder."

Coach shook his head. "No, brother. It's as if I've walked the same path before. Because I have. Peter, I know you want to be a good leader. You want to develop great people. And this is a method that will work. I can promise you that. Meet with them one on one. It's like with me—I want to develop and keep great players. So I meet with them one on one. It worked. I'm still here, aren't I?"

"Yeah, you are."

"So let's talk about how to do the one-on-one meetings. They have to be done correctly, so that your people don't get the idea that this is just one more thing on your list to check off."

Coach O moved to the "How To" section of the newsletter. "I love how he broke this down for both coaches and business leaders. I'll read the coach's section first and then you read the business leader portion. As you listen closely to my section, remember that I've done *all* of this. *This* is what turned things around for me and my team."

Coach O took a deep breath and read aloud.

SPORT COACHES: Over the last decade, I have found the most optimal frequency of meetings between players and coaches is a minimum of three meetings when in-season and one per month in the off-season (with weekly texts woven in).

In-Season One-on-One Meeting Schedule:

1. Execute three weeks into the season. (This way, you and the player can evaluate: performance, possible roles, and their personal life. For example, "How is life going for you personally now that you are roughly a month in?"
2. Execute just after the midpoint of the season and discuss the same things as above, with more emphasis on the role they are finding themselves in or you want them to pursue.
3. Execute one week prior to the conference tournament, playoffs, or final game. Note: This is *not* an exit interview. At this point, you will discuss everything listed in the

meetings above and their role in the upcoming games, as it may have changed due to injury, etc.

Coach stopped and looked up at Peter. "I want you to underline this. I did this exactly as he describes it here, and within the first season, things changed dramatically. Enough that I kept my job." He handed the newsletter to Peter. "Your turn."

Peter took it, glanced over the section, then read it, stumbling over a few words.

BUSINESS LEADERS/EXECS: Over the last decade, I have found the most optimal frequency of one-on-one meetings between executives and team members is a minimum of one time per month and additional quarterly reviews.

Coaching Points: I would perform both on-site and off-site one-on-ones with my team members. At least once quarterly I would take the team member off-site, perhaps for a short coffee meeting as a changeup.

Quote to Remember: "No one should ever be surprised that they are being let go or fired."

Peter handed the newsletter back to Coach.

"The next section, Peter, is an important outline on how to run these meetings so your people will know you're being sincere in your concern for them." He read on.

Here's three simple things to remember for the format of your meetings:

The Three Ps: Give them these at the start of every meeting as a way to explain what you want to accomplish. *Purpose, Process, and Payoff.* People don't like to be ambushed, so start with the **Purpose** of the meeting, which is to give them clarity on everything and help them grow professionally and personally.

The Process: Discuss what they are doing well. Next, ask them how their life is and how they like playing or working at _____? Ask them to rate their professional life on a scale of 1-10 (one being horrible and ten being awesome). Finally ask them: "How can I help you move your score closer to a ten?" Then both of you come to an agreement on what the OBT (or One Big Thing) you and they will be working on together in the days ahead.

The Payoff: Ask them to tell you their one takeaway from this meeting. Your people should walk away from this meeting with great clarity and you need to make sure they are taking away the right thing. Remember high clarity creates high performance.

The biggest mistake I see coaches and execs make in their one-on-one meetings is to not make the team members state, verbally, what they are expected to do moving forward. Or worse, the team member states the wrong thing or too many things, and the leader doesn't bring them back to the main thing or their one big thing.

Coach looked up. "Peter, people need to feel safe, secure, and significant. Hunt what they are doing well first and remind them of why you recruited or hired them. Then, give them only one big thing (OBT) to work on, not three or even two.

Finally, they must feel like you are here to help them and are in it with them. After all, you are either coaching them or letting their lack of improvement happen."

Coach changed positions in the chair and his voice lowered, becoming even more serious. "Peter, earlier you mentioned not having time. A lot of people think this way, but when done correctly, one-on-one meetings can be one of the most powerful motivation tools you can utilize. But leaders often don't do them, primarily complaining about a lack of time and control over the content of the meetings."

At Peter's look of surprise, Coach smiled. "Yeah, big surprise that headstrong and hardworking leaders want to control things. Yes, people are messy and at times require high maintenance. So are we; we just forget that we're also human and flawed. But in the 21st century, we can't afford not to stay out in front of things. You simply can't wait until the end of the year or season. Your people want clarity and relationship.

"Don't get me wrong. You don't need to be their buddy or even a close friend to do a one-on-one meeting. This is still about business. To be in relationship, you don't have to hang out together. You still need to be their coach and mentor. There is much more to talk about on this topic and the art of the one-on-one meeting, but hopefully this gives you enough information to help you move forward in helping your people be the best they can be.

"Speaking of time, when you schedule one-on-one meetings, give yourself a set amount of time. I find 40-60 minutes optimal; 20-30 is probably too short and anything over 60 minutes—well, someone is talking too much."

They both laughed, and Peter let out a long breath. "This is a lot to keep in mind."

"It is, but remember this is a process, not an event. You will be having more than one meeting with them. You will build trust and rapport, and that will happen over time, not during the first meeting. That one may be a little awkward but give it a chance." Coach picked up the newsletter. "I always tell them I am going to ask them some questions and see where they lead. I tell them I am not a lawyer, a priest, or a counselor so if they tell me they are a serial killer or have broken a law, I will have to report it. Otherwise, these meetings are built on trust. Everything said in them is strictly confidential, just between the two of you.

My hope is that they will always walk away feeling more connected to me, have greater clarity, and be inspired when they leave the room.

Any questions so far?"

Peter, who had been scribbling as Coach talked, finished writing and looked up. "Just one."

"Shoot."

"What do you do if the person you are meeting with doesn't comply? I mean, what if they're not all in? Do you know what I mean?" Peter sat back in his chair.

"I sure do. Remember, I coach 17- to 23-year-olds. They can be masters at 'not being all in.' The best thing you can do for that type of person is to be honest and straightforward about the expectations of the one-on-one meetings. Full participation, honesty, and trust are non-negotiable. Peter, there's one more thing that may be helpful here. Lock this in and write it down: *People are messy.*"

Peter grinned. "We sure are."

Coach O smiled and then pulled from his notebook a 3 x 5 notecard and handed it to Peter. "This is a copy of my notes from one of my player meetings. It may help you as a reference point. I use it as a guide to keep me on track for each meeting. Take this and tweak it for your own one-on-ones. Instead of being aimed at sports and team staff, you can tweak it for your executive team and your staff and your particular business."

As Peter looked at the card, he loved the simplicity and clarity of the reminders.

One-on-One Player Meeting Progression

1. Give them the three Ps of the meeting

2. Tell them two things you really like about them that you've seen in preseason workouts.

3. Tell them why you recruited them and how you've seen that come through so far (start communicating what their role is).

4. State the "One Big Thing" you want them to get better at before Game 1.

5. Have them restate numbers 3 & 4 back to you. Tell them you love 'em and glad they are playing for you.

"Thank you for this. For all of this."

The men stood, and Coach O put his hand on Peter's shoulder.

"The purpose of these meetings is to connect with people and help them discover answers for themselves so they can grow. It's not about fixing people like a lawnmower or a computer.

It's not even about making you more likeable. These meetings are about helping your team make a change in their mindset and/or behavior. You can't make someone change; they must want to grow.

Remember, you aren't a repairman, you are a gardener.

Be a great 'question asker' and if you listen well, your employees may teach or help you more than you help them."

As they shook hands, Coach reminded him, "You have a lot to process. Call me and let me know how things are progressing. I'll also check in when I get a chance."

"I will." Peter headed to his Jeep, a new excitement building in his chest. He had a goal and a plan to make it happen. As his phone connected to his SUV, he called Gabrielle. Time to set up some appointments.

CHAPTER 5
Truth over Tradition

Peter set the first team meeting for three that afternoon, and he forwarded the information from the *Harvard Business Review* to each of his executives. He wanted to give them time to read and absorb the details while he reviewed the files on each of them. He wanted to have firmly in his mind why he had brought them to the company, as well as the nature of his relationship to them. He started notes for each of them.

Next, Peter checked his calendar for openings. He'd ask Gabrielle to handle the final appointments, but he wanted to see how fast he could work these into his schedule. He wanted to meet with Mark first. The minute Coach had mentioned starting the one-on-one meetings, Peter knew Mark needed a private meeting more than any of the others.

As Chief Operations Officer, Mark's broad range of duties reached into almost every area of the company. Most everyone in the company knew Mark, but his likeability scores were almost as flat as Peter's own. Mark worked hard—he was at the office almost as much as Peter was—and he'd been instrumental in some major changes over the past two years. Mark was one of the major reasons that the company was running at a leaner, more efficient level.

But Peter wondered if some cracks weren't beginning to appear. He made a note to meet with Mark first thing tomorrow morning.

Peter then went down the list of his team, making similar notes on the other five: the CFO, as well as the four Executive Vice Presidents: Legal, Retail and Vendor Management, Research and Development, and Marketing and Publicity. These six people were the core of the company, and if Coach was right, bringing them on board with this thought process would cause a cascade of change.

A much-needed cascade of change.

Finally, Peter took out Coach's notecard and studied it. He would definitely need to adapt it for his own needs, and after a few minutes, he drafted a new one:

One-on-One Executive Meeting Progression

1. Give them the three Ps of the meeting

2. Tell them why you hired them and how you've seen that come through so far (start communicating what their role is).

3. Ask them how they like working here on a scale of (1-10)
* Ask how you could help them raise the evaluation number?
3a. Ask them how their work/life balance is on a 1-10 scale?
* Ask how you could help them raise the evaluation number?

4. State the "One Big Thing" you want them to get better at this month or quarter.

5. Have them restate number 4 back to you.
* Tell them you Love 'em and are so glad they are working with you.

Peter compared it with Coach's card, his own notes, and the newsletter. Satisfied that it provided a workable model, Peter leaned back in his chair with a sigh. This wasn't going to be an easy path, but definitely the right one. He prayed his team would understand it.

Precisely at three, the team gathered with uncharacteristic quiet in Peter's office. As they headed for the conference table, he redirected them to the sitting area. They exchanged worried looks as they settled. Mark looked the most concerned.

"You have nothing to worry about." Peter settled in his chair, facing them. "This is not about your jobs. The purpose of this meeting is to discuss how we manage our teams, and some of the changes we need to make. It's about how we communicate now, and the best ways to process information through the company in the future. It's also about the need for more one-on-one meetings, eliminating the yearly reviews, and how that will improve our vision as well as the relationships with our employees on all levels.

"As you saw in the information I sent yesterday regarding yearly reviews, employees today need much more interaction with us. They want—and need—clear expectations and feedback, and with yearly reviews it's too much information too late. They just aren't enough anymore. People see a monthly one-on-one meeting as an opportunity to connect with us and feel more valued by the company.

"We need to focus on the truth of what really works more than a traditional mindset. We need to move to a method of having one-on-one monthly meetings and quarterly reviews.

The truth is, the traditional process of only a once-a-year review is not only outdated, it's ineffective in producing greater performance results.

We want our people to have great clarity of the expectations we have of them, and we want them to feel valued as we give them timely feedback and coaching along the way."

Peter then handed out copies of the newsletter and detailed what he'd learned from Coach O. He explained about the one-on-ones he would set up with each of them, and the expectation each of them would do the same with their direct reports.

"We need to establish a cascade of information, from the top of the company on down.

We need to build and encourage our relationships, and—most of all—we need to listen, really listen, to what our people are saying."

As he spoke, Peter watched for reactions. Most members of his team seemed thoughtful, just taking it all in, the way he had with Coach O. Such a change did take a bit of processing, a time to let all the details ferment. But their questions were sound and based on their understanding of the corporate vision, an encouraging sign.

Except for Mark, who remained silent. He focused on the newsletter, but his gaze was distant, a 1,000-yard stare. Peter definitely needed to meet with him first.

As the questions wound down, Peter reminded them that Gabrielle would be setting up the meetings with each of them over the next few days. They left, and Peter could hear the chatter starting up in the hallway. Another good sign. But he couldn't shake the feeling that something else was going on with Mark, something that needed to be addressed as soon as possible.

When Mark arrived at Peter's office the next morning at 8:30, the shadows around his eyes and the tension in his face revealed his sleepless night and concern over this meeting. Even before Peter had shut the door, Mark crossed his arms and squared his shoulders. "I know my likeability scores have bottomed out."

Peter paused, then moved two of the more comfortable chairs so that they were at a slight angle to each other. He gestured to the coffee setup Gabrielle had left on an accent table. "Coffee?"

Mark hesitated, then poured a cup of steaming, black coffee.

"Sit," Peter said. "And know that we are not here to talk about anyone's scores. Although I will tell you that mine are even worse than yours."

Mark sat, looking up at his CEO. "Seriously?"

Peter nodded as he poured his own cup of coffee. "Rock bottom. But today, that's not even on the agenda." He set the coffee down and pulled the 3 x 5 card from his pocket.

"This meeting is about me hearing you. The main purpose of the meeting is to make sure we're clear on what you want to do to grow professionally and personally as well as what the company expects from you.

It's to help us connect better and have greater clarity on expectations, in addition to helping you be the best version of yourself, to maximize your potential, and help you reach your dreams.

I want to know what's working for you and what's not. I want us to agree on one big thing you want to achieve this quarter. And I want us to leave today with complete transparency on all expectations. Does this make sense?"

Mark took a sip of coffee, then set the cup aside. "It does, although I'm not exactly sure how to start."

"Let's begin with the basics. On a scale of 1 to 10, how do you like working here?" When Mark hesitated, Peter leaned forward, his voice dropping. "Mark, I want us to be honest with each other. Again, your job is not on the line with this, and what's said in these meetings is completely confidential."

Mark shifted in his chair. "OK. Look, I like the company. The people are great, and it's one of the best jobs I've had. But if I had to put a number on it, I'd say a seven."

Peter nodded. "Not bad. Now tell me what it would take to make it an eight?"

Mark stared at his boss, his eyes wider with curiosity. "Truthfully?"

"Absolutely."

He paused, then seemed to dive into the process with more enthusiasm. "This is an old building. We're fighting to keep all the zones an even temp. The facilities manager thinks there's mold in parts of the warehouse. I need at least two more people to work with him on getting things fixed and updated, and we need to have the warehouse inspected. And a night manager would be a great help. Some things that go pop in the night can't wait till the next day for attention."

"What else?"

"Can I send you a list?"

"Please do. So you've been trying to juggle this with everything else that's going on?"

"Yes, sir."

"And you're on call?"

"I am, 24/7."

"So the phone rings at all hours and you're here more than you're at home."

"That's about the size of it."

"So, on a scale of one to ten, how is your work/home balance?"

Mark stilled, obviously caught off guard by the change in topic. He reached for his cup, and Peter waited. The cup clinked hard on the tray as Mark replaced it.

"That good, huh?" Peter asked quietly.

Mark took a deep breath. "Maybe a five. Possibly a four."

"That's trouble brewing." When Mark remained silent, Peter said, "How can I help?"

Mark shrugged, staring at his hands. "I'm not sure."

Peter pressed further. "What can we do to lighten your responsibilities here?" Mark remained silent, and Peter took a deep breath. "Mark, the goal here is to improve our relationships across the board. With our employees, with each other, with our families. I know I've got a lot of work to do at home as well."

Mark glanced sideways at him. "You do?"

"Oh, yeah. I've let work consume me the last two years. My drive to improve things here resulted in me letting things go at home. Mary seems to stay mad at me most days, and my son has stopped speaking to us. Sara just turned 14 and I don't even know how to reach her anymore."

Mark straightened. "I know what you mean. I feel like every meal has been interrupted. Beth has given up on us, I think. And my son finds every excuse on the planet not to be in the same room. I feel as if I'm losing them."

"What would you like to do to make it better?"

Enthusiasm suddenly lit Mark's eyes, and he turned more toward Peter. "Our pastor has suggested that all couples invest in a 'date night.' You know, make plans, go out, just the two of you, do something that's fun. Like when before we were married. He also suggested that we do it, individually, with each of the kids. Beth and I talked about it, and we'd love to do it, but . . ." His voice trailed off.

"But you haven't had an uninterrupted meal in months."

Mark nodded. "It feels like years."

Peter had an idea. "So . . . what if one night every weekend, we take you off call. If something happens, your phone would roll to your second-in-command. Or even third-in-command. They can handle most things, right?"

Mark almost leaped out of his chair. "They can! Extremely qualified folks. Are you serious about this? Man, that would be awesome!"

Peter was a bit surprised at the change in Mark's mood. Had he really let things get this bad for his employees? "Yes, I mean it. Mark, brother . . . you're a valued part of this organization. I looked over your file yesterday, and you have an astonishing resume. We'd be idiots to lose you because we put too much on you. And, yes, I'll look into the budget to see if we have room for a third-shift facilities manager."

Mark's excitement was palpable. "That's almost too much to ask for!"

"Well . . ."

"But I wouldn't turn it down!"

Peter laughed. "OK, we'll see what we can do. You talk to your team about who's up for being on call once a month, and we'll do some rotation on the on-call status. Now, I want to talk about one more thing."

"OK."

"Other than what we just talked about, what is one thing you'd like to accomplish that you haven't had a chance to work on?"

Mark didn't hesitate. "Training."

Peter's eyebrows arched. "How so?"

"Peter, we have some amazing people on our team, with a lot of potential. But they don't know how things work, either here in the company or the industry at large. I'd love to set up a few training sessions, maybe even a few 'learn at lunch' sessions, to get them familiar with what's possible and what they'd need to take their careers to the next step."

"You don't think you'd be training them to leave?"

"Not if we stayed on top of it, with opportunities for them to advance here."

Peter thought about it for a minute. "That's a good idea. Put a plan together—times, topics, teachers—and do an ROI statement about it for our next meeting. That can be your OBT for this month?"

"OBT?"

"One Big Thing. I want everyone to leave our monthly meetings with a single item to focus on for the next month.

Your training plan can be your OBT this month. Agreed?"

Mark nodded. "So my OBT this month is the plan for employee training and advance, including the logistics and ROI statement."

"Works for me. Is there anything else I can do for you this next month?"

Mark let out a long breath. "I don't think so. I'm still stunned about this much."

Peter stood and Mark did as well. "Mark, never let things get this out of control again. We have to support each other." Peter held out his hand to shake Mark's.

Mark took his hand, then impulsively pulled Peter into a hug. "Thank you, Peter. This means the world to me." He released Peter as suddenly as he'd grabbed him.

Peter almost stumbled backwards but caught himself. He started to speak, then notice the glistening in Mark's eyes. Tears. Peter's chest tightened.

One meeting. One meeting made all the difference.

He clapped Mark on the shoulder. "I just wish we'd done this months ago." He closed the door behind his COO and dropped back into his chair. He only had three more of the one-on-ones scheduled for today, and Peter realized that might be a blessing.

If all the meetings were this intense, he thought, it's going to be a long day. Impactful and powerful. . . but long. And he was about to learn more about his team, his company, and himself—more than he ever thought possible.

The remaining three one-on-one meetings that day were intense and almost as compelling as Mark's. Beneficial, informational, and—to Peter's surprise—full of hope. By four, he felt energized instead of exhausted. This could really turn things around.

As Peter returned to the chair behind his desk, Gabrielle walked in to remind him of his one-on-one with Naomi.

"Ah, yes." He'd forgotten that he and Gabrielle had added this meeting to the schedule late yesterday to accommodate Naomi's travel schedule.

"Thank you, Gabrielle. How long before she's up?" He needed some time to recalibrate and recapture some energy.

Gabrielle walked over to the sitting area and grabbed the empty coffee carafe. "Thirty minutes." She made a turn for the door with the coffee carafe.

"Gabrielle?"

She turned to face him. "Yes."

"Do you have a few minutes?" Peter walked over and took the coffee carafe from her and placed it on the table, then motioned toward one of the chairs. "Please, sit."

Nervously, Gabrielle slid into the chair, choosing a short-term posture.

Peter sat in the chair opposite her. "How long have we known each other?"

"Nearly a decade."

"Other than my wife, you know me better than anyone. Can I ask you for some feedback? I mean, about me. As a leader, here at the office."

Gabrielle repositioned herself in the chair as she formed her answer. "Peter, I'm just your assistant . . ."

Peter interrupted her, "No, Gabrielle. You are the gatekeeper of my life and at times this entire company. You have a perspective of me and how people view me that I need to hear. I trust you and your position here is secure. I need you to tell me the truth. Please?"

Gabrielle unknowingly sat up and leaned forward. "The truth?"

"Yes, and let's start with people's perception of me, specifically the exec team. And I'm not asking you to use names; just give me their perspective from your viewpoint. Oh, and this is confidential. It won't leave this room."

She decided to tell him. "Sir . . ."

"Peter, please."

"Peter." She took a deep breath. "Most people who work closely with you admire you and your work ethic. They know you don't mean to disregard them so often."

Peter interrupted, "Disregard?"

"Yes. Do you know how many times a week I am forced to reschedule meetings with your staff and other people?"

Peter shook his head.

"At least five times per week, roughly one a day. And when people come in to just stop by for your opinion or to give you an idea, you . . . well, you're very short with them and rarely look at them when they speak to you, and this makes them feel like you are brushing them off.

I mean, it's like whatever you're doing is way more important than them."

It stung, but Peter kept writing down notes. Gabrielle, now gaining confidence pushed on. "When I have to reschedule meetings constantly, it makes you look disorganized and worse, it makes everyone else feel like you don't want to make time for them and don't value them or their thoughts. And if I'm being honest, I'm tired of having to tell people you need to reschedule or can't make it."

Peter finished writing and looked up. "What about you?"

Gabrielle's eyes met his then dropped, followed by her head. She reached for a napkin on the table and brought it toward her bowed head and wiped the small tears from her cheeks. As she began to speak again, her head started to come up. "Peter, I'm forever grateful for this job and the opportunity to serve you and the other execs here, but at times it's like you have no clue how difficult life can be for people other than you. I'm a single mom trying to raise my two kids and, well . . . do you even know my kids' ages?"

Peter felt his heart pounding; he didn't know their ages. He had an idea, but had to admit he did not. How could he be so shallow and self-absorbed? She'd been working for him for ten years! "I'm sorry, Gabrielle. I have an idea but I'm not sure."

"That's okay. They're 13 and 15 now. Anyway, my point is that we all have busy lives and if you're asking my opinion..

You give others the feeling that their lives and schedules just aren't as important as yours.

There, I said it. Sorry." She folded the moist napkin into a small square while looking down.

"No need for apologies, Gabrielle. I asked for and need the truth. Especially from you. Do you have any suggestions?"

"Yes sir—I mean Peter. If you could just keep your appointments, number one. If we need to put more buffer time between appointments, just let me know, but I can't keep covering for you all the time. It hurts your credibility as a leader. Also, when people just stop by to say hello or share an idea, could you please stop what you're doing, look them in the eye and give them your undivided attention? All they want to do is please you and earn your respect."

Peter had stopped writing and was locking in everything she was saying. "Anything else?"

"No, I mean . . ."

"Go ahead, Gabrielle. I trust you and your opinion. Tell me, what is it?"

"It's just that you don't acknowledge the people of service in the company. The secretaries, delivery people, and especially the custodians. These people say hello to you daily and play such an important part of our culture here.

I've heard you say in the past that great leaders value everyone and make everyone feel valued. These people don't want gifts or raises. They just want the boss not to treat them like they're invisible.

That's all."

This time Peter kept his head down and was pretending to write. *Invisible.* That one hurt.

How did he become the boss he always vowed he never would be?

Gabrielle stood up and grabbed the carafe again. "Well, Naomi will be coming in soon and I'd better get this refilled."

Peter stood up and spoke. "Gabrielle." He walked toward her, stopped and looked her in the eyes. "Gabrielle, thank you. I am so, so sorry. Thank you for having the courage to speak the truth to me. I know that couldn't have been easy for you."

Gabrielle fidgeted in place.

"I can't be a better man and leader if I don't know the truth. You know what they say: A lack of self-awareness is the number one killer of executives today.

This meeting ended up being the most important one of my day, and with your help I want to implement the changes you suggested. Also, if you're open to it, I would like us to have a scheduled one-on-one every month to benefit the both of us. Thank you."

"I would be honored, sir. I mean Peter." They both laughed.

As Gabrielle lifted the coffee carafe again, she smiled and said, "I'll see if Naomi is here yet." Then she turned and walked toward the door, still smiling.

* * * *

Peter's meeting with Naomi went well. Another impactful exchange, and she even reiterated some of the things Gabrielle had said in a very roundabout manner. They would have to work on their ability to speak more directly with each other, but Naomi was another rock star and he looked forward to future meetings with her.

As he strode out of the building, Peter pulled out his phone and sent Mary a text to let her know he was on the way home. No need to scare her half to death by showing up at home early.

Peter was exhausted, but the trip home felt lighter than it had since he'd first taken over the CEO position years ago. Coach O had been right. Peter didn't yet understand *why*, but he desperately hoped they could maintain the momentum created by the one-on-one meetings. He knew it would take a great deal of work and intentionality, but he also knew he had to continue on this path. He thought again about Mark's ideas on training and coaching for the company leaders, wondering if Coach O might be available for a session or two. It could be a boon for the entire company if everyone could hear these ideas.

CHAPTER 6
Out of the Mouths of Babes

The brainstorming continued as he pulled into the garage and lowered the door. As he got out, he idly noticed that Sara's pink cruising bike was missing from the rack. *Must be out for a ride.* He pushed open the door, his enthusiasm bubbling over.

"Mary! Sweetheart!"

His wife stood at the stove, her back to him. Peter launched into his planned announcement without stopping.

"You won't believe what happened today! Coach was so spot on! Those meetings, they are going to change everything. What a difference—"

He stopped as Mary turned. Mascara streaked down her face, and red blotches covered her skin. Tears glistened in her eyes and poured down her cheeks.

"Mary! What's wrong? Honey!" He reached for her.

She stopped him, and her words were harsh and clogged from crying. "It's Sara! She's gone!"

He didn't quite believe what he was hearing. "What do you mean, 'She's gone'?" He pulled a chair from under the kitchen table and eased her down into it. "When? Why?"

Mary sat, swallowing hard. Peter pulled his handkerchief from his inside coat pocket and pressed it into her hands. "We had a fight."

"About what?"

Mary wiped her face, smearing the mascara even more. She sniffed, then glared at him. "About you."

"Me? Why?"

"She wants me to divorce you since you obviously don't love any of us."

Peter's knees gave away and he knelt in front of Mary. *Dear God, help me.* "But you know that's not true."

Mary sniffed and wiped her eyes again.

"Actions speak louder than words, Peter."

Peter couldn't get his breath, and his words came out as a whisper. "Where is she?"

His wife shook her head. "I don't know. She took her bike. I'd gotten your text, so I didn't go after her." She paused. "I didn't want you to come home to a silent house and not know where we were. I didn't think you'd get a text in time."

The ache in Peter's chest spread. "Mary, I love you and I always have." She nodded, and he kissed her forehead. "I'll find her. I promise. Stay here, just in case, but I'll find her."

Peter grabbed his keys and headed out, racking his brain for ideas. *Where would she go?* Back to the school. Maybe too far. Just riding? The neighborhood wasn't that big. Eventually she'd come to one of the "big roads," which had always terrified her.

But was she still terrified of them? He desperately hoped so. The image of Sara biking along a four-lane sent a new spike of fear through him. Why didn't he know? How long had it been since they'd ridden bikes together? Or done anything together as a family? At least with him along? Months?

Years?

Peter's phone buzzed. *Maybe she's gone home?* He answered.

"Peter? Are you busy? How did the meetings go?"

Coach O. Peter had forgotten to call him.

"Coach. I can't talk right now. Sara has disappeared."

"What? When?"

"This afternoon. She and Mary got into a fight and she bolted on her bike. I'm looking for her now."

"Do you need help?"

"Lord, I hope not. I'm praying she's still in the neighborhood."

"I'll be praying too. Call me when you know something. And I have something else I need to share with you."

"Will do. Later."

As Peter ended the call, what he'd said to Coach rang true. He did hope Sara was still on the neighborhood streets she knew well. But where? Friends? The local park...

Peter braked, a memory flashing through his mind. They'd just moved to the neighborhood. Sara had only been four, and Peter was the one to introduce her to the community's park. How many times had they made the journey on their bikes, especially when Sara and Mary would get into it, one of their mother-daughter spats? Sara would flee to her father, looking for support and respite.

From the time they'd moved, Peter had always been Sara's "safe place." She turned to him whenever the new school made her crazy or Aaron had gotten on her last nerve. As the teen years hit and conflicts with her mother escalated, Sara had always turned to him. He'd never taken her side over Mary's, but he'd been able to diffuse most fights with a quick trip to the park and the swings. Sara loved the swings.

Higher, Daddy. Push me higher!

Peter turned the Jeep and headed for the park. He spotted the bike first, its pink frame shining, even as the afternoon light began to dim. It stood near the swings, where Sara sat, pushing back and forth with one foot, her toe twisting in the soft sand below.

Relief rushed through him. Peter parked and headed for the swings slowly, as if he expected her to run when she saw him. In a way, he did. After all, he had not been there for her in months. She now had as many fights with him as she did with Mary.

How had he let this special child drift so far away?

He swallowed the lump in his throat. "Sara?"

She kept staring at the ground. "I guess I have to run away to get your attention."

"No, you don't." He sat down in the swing next to her. "But I don't blame you for thinking that."

"I thought Mom would be the one to find me."

"Even though I'm the reason you fought?"

Sara kicked her foot harder against the ground, making her swing spin. "Yeah. You're never around anymore. You're never home till midnight." She glanced at him, then back at the ground. "What are you even doing home this time of day anyway?"

"To apologize."

She stopped her swing. "Saying 'I'm sorry,' isn't enough, Daddy. You say that a lot. It doesn't mean anything."

"I know. I need to change. Because I don't want to lose any of you."

Sara finally looked up at him. "Mom told you what I said?"

"Yes. You're wrong. I love all of you more than anything else in the world. But I can understand why you'd think I didn't."

"Yeah, right. Another apology. I'm so tired of all that. You gonna do more this time than say sorry and try to buy us stuff? I hate the bribes, Daddy."

"No more bribes. No more sorrys. Today is the first day of a big change. Give me a chance?"

She shrugged and looked at the ground again. "You got lots to make up for. Y'know?"

"I know. And I want to know more about what you want from me."

Sara rolled her eyes. "You're my dad. What do you think I want?"

Peter took a deep breath. No one said this would be easy. "How about if I just start being more of a dad? Like being there for you, and your brother and mom?"

"It'll take more than just being there. Anyone can just show up." She scowled. "Even you if you try. You gotta really *be there*. Like . . . *for* us. Not just *with* us. *Daddy*." She turned the last word into four syllables, then shrugged again.

"Talk to us. Listen. Maybe even put down your phone once in a while."

Peter grinned. "I will if you will."

Sara snickered. "Fair."

"How about if I promise all of you that I'll work on pulling the family back together?"

Another shrug. "We're not little kids anymore. We got lots going on. And we don't trust you. You got a lot to make up for if you want us to listen again."

"Then I'll have to work harder than I did before. Especially on the listening part. And I'll need your help."

Sara straightened and faced him. "Aaron ain't gonna be easy."

Peter fought the urge to smile. Aaron would probably be easier than this teenager, who was beginning to see things with more adult eyes. He held out his hand. "Go back with me?"

After a moment, she nodded, and took his hand. Peter grabbed her bike as they headed to the Jeep. He opened the tailgate and put her bike in the back and after they both got in and put their seat belts on, Sara grabbed her dad's hand and put her head on his shoulder for a few seconds. Peter didn't say a word; he just squeezed his daughter's hand and they headed back to the house.

Mary had washed her face and had started the makings of a spaghetti dinner. Sara apologized to her mother, and they hugged, even though Mary said she'd kill her daughter if Sara ever scared them that way again. Sara giggled at the mock threat and headed to her room.

Dinner was a quiet affair, and Peter's announcement that he wanted to have a family meeting at eight brought only mildly surprised looks. Aaron, who still had not spoken to Peter, merely shrugged.

As Mary and Peter cleaned the kitchen, he asked if Aaron had said anything to Mary at all. She shook her head.

"Nope. I think he may talk to Sara, but she won't admit it. She's loyal." Mary paused. "You know he probably thinks you're going to announce our divorce."

Peter reached and pulled his wife into a hug. "I'm sorry I let it get this bad. I know you've tried to run interference for me with them."

She returned the hug, leaning against him. "Just don't do it again, mister."

He chuckled. After they finished, he headed up to his home office to prepare for the family meeting, still unsure how he would approach the changes he wanted to make on the home front. The way he'd conducted the one-on-one meetings at the office probably wouldn't be as effective.

His phone buzzed and he picked it up. Coach O. *Oops.* He'd forgotten again. "Hey, Coach. I'm sorry. I found her, but it's been a little tense around here. Now I'm trying to prepare for a family meeting. I've got a lot of things to fix."

"So my timing is perfect."

"How so?"

"Because what you need to do is not about 'fixing' anything. It's about gaining wisdom and making behavior changes that are lasting.

You cannot 'fix' what happened in the past. That's over. Apologies won't heal anything unless the situation and your behavior changes. They're hollow without real differences in how you behave toward your family."

Peter took a deep breath. "I know. I've said so many sorrys that they're meaningless. So how do I start?"

"Start by asking them three questions. I call them the three questions of truth. That way you will get honest answers and true feedback about what's going on in your home. Are you ready to write something down?"

Peter pulled a notebook out of a drawer and grabbed a pen. "Go."

"Give each of them a sheet of paper with these three questions:

What are the things you love that I do? What are the things that I need to stop doing immediately? What would you like to see me do more of?"

Peter scribbled furiously. "Got it."

"Read them back to me." After Peter did, Coach continued. "Don't make them answer tonight. Give them time to think about the questions. Collect them in a day or two. When you read the answers, be prepared to be hurt, even angry. Just keep in mind that this is not about you. It's about them and their feelings. Instead of reacting, study them. Look for a central theme. Believe me, you'll find a common thread that runs through all the answers. Tell them you want to meet with them again, then call me."

Peter put down the pen. "Tell me this is the hard part."

Coach laughed. "Just the beginning, brother. It's just the beginning."

CHAPTER 7
Tell Me What I Need to Hear... Not What I Want to Hear

Peter stood in the den, looking at his family. Aaron had scrunched into his usual corner of the sectional, knees drawn up, eyes on his phone, although he didn't fit quite as well as he used to. Mary sat next to her son, occasionally touching his leg in a gesture of affection and reassurance. Sara sat on the opposite side of the couch, texting furiously. Her favorite color had recently shifted from pink to purple, and her pajamas looked as if they belonged in a 1960s rock club.

Peter held out his hand to her. With a scowl, she put her phone in his palm. When he stepped toward Aaron, his son tossed his phone at Mary. She barely caught it, then set it to one side.

His stomach queasy, Peter began. "I know things have been tough—"

Sara snorted, and Aaron shot her a grin.

Peter paused, glancing from one to the other. They glared back. Time for a different tactic.

"This is not about what you expect. Your mother and I are not getting a divorce." They both looked away, but Peter pressed on. "Mary has been my best friend and my only love since we were eighteen. That has not changed. We vowed to be together for a lifetime, and we both took that vow seriously."

Sara peered at him from under her long lashes. Aaron looked at his mother, who smiled sweetly at her son, then her husband.

"That's right. We still love each other, and I love each of you, even though I've been a pretty bad husband lately. And a lousy father. I'm not going to apologize because, as Sara pointed out to me, I've done that so much lately it doesn't mean much. Not without some changes being made. So what I want to do tonight is to promise all of you that changes are being made. Here. And at work. It's not going to be easy. I've developed some bad habits."

He paused again. "And I need your help."

"We haven't done anything wrong," Sara muttered.

"No, you haven't. But you and Aaron are changing too, growing up. Just the fact that you're now a teen, and Aaron will be in a few months, means that your place in this house—and in the rest of your life—will shift. You'll have more responsibility. School will demand more of you. More than ever, we need to pull together as a family. Support each other. Lift each other up. We can't keep pulling apart into our own spaces."

Sara's expression turned defiant. "And whose fault is that?"

"Mine."

The word hung in the air a moment. "So I need to make some changes. I need to take the lead in this. But I need your help as well."

Mary leaned forward. "What do you need from us?"

"Instructions."

Aaron finally looked up at him, which Peter took as a good sign. He picked up three pieces of paper from the coffee table. "There are three questions on these: *What do you like that I do? What do I need to stop doing immediately? What do you want me to do more of or start doing?* I want you to answer each question honestly, from your heart. No matter how bad it may seem, I need to hear the truth from you, and not what you think I want to hear. Not even what I may think I want to hear. The truth."

"You won't like it." Sara shifted and crossed her arms.

"Probably not. But this isn't about me or what I like. It's about you. And you don't have to answer them tonight. Just in the next couple of days. Leave them on my desk. Are you busy Thursday night?"

Mary cleared her throat. "Sara has ballet after school. Aaron has robotics club. We should be home by 5:30."

"So . . . meet this same time Thursday night?" One by one, they each nodded. He handed them the papers, then paused. "And I hope, someday, you can forgive me."

Without the usual prayer Peter had always used to end their family meetings, he turned and left the room, giving them space and time in a room that had always been their safe, family space. He prayed that much had not changed.

On Wednesday, he finished the one-on-one meetings with the last two members of his executive team. Mark and the three executives he'd met with on Tuesday had already begun their own one-on-ones, and information about the desired changes in reports and evaluations had already started to cascade downward. After lunch, Gabrielle filled him in on the information that had flooded the middle management level of the company about the one-on-one meetings. So far, the reactions had been positive, although some employees still had doubts.

"You think they'll come around?" Peter asked.

She shrugged. "Some people are always going to gripe. But yes, I think most will. They seem to like the idea of having more input, more often, into how things are going around here."

The rest of the afternoon was a return to normal business concerns, and Peter embraced them. He did love his job, and he hoped the changes he made would help him keep it. By the time he got home, Mary had started dinner and the kids had retreated to their rooms. A touch of normalcy. Peter realized he had not asked his wife about her own job in more than a week. After he changed into sweats, he asked if he could help with dinner, and she eagerly put him to work.

"So, how are things at your job?" He tried to sound casual, but Mary started laughing.

"What's so funny?"

She put down the knife she used to chop vegetables and faced him.

"Peter, I love you. But if you do an about-face like this all of a sudden, you'll give us all whiplash."

He leaned against the counter, trying to ignore how much her comment hurt. "Was I really that bad?"

"Yep." She went to him and slid her arms around his waist. "What's even worse? We had almost gotten used to it. Just the way you were. The way things had to be. We all found our own ways to cope. I admire what you're doing, and I love you for it. But give us time. All right?"

"Wow." He hugged her tighter. "Thank you."

"For what?"

"Not giving up on me."

Mary pushed back a bit and looked into his face. "Do you remember, when we were just married, how we went out to that one drive-in movie left in the area? Almost every Saturday night. Bad movies, but—"

"—the best popcorn on the planet."

"Dinner and movie for less than ten bucks. Perfect for our budget back then."

"Yeah?"

She touched his nose.

"I still remember that man. That version of Peter. I just prayed God would help you find your way back.

I didn't know He'd use Coach O to do it, but I'm grateful."

"But you need time."

"All of us do. And, by the way, your answers to those questions are already on your desk."

"Really?"

"And I suspect you need to do that instead of peeling potatoes. Dinner will be ready in about an hour."

"Thank you." He kissed her, then headed out of the kitchen. He stopped when she called his name.

"And, Peter?"

"Yes?"

"My job is fine. Smooth as glass." She grinned. "We'll talk later."

He saluted her and headed to his office, where he found all three sheets of paper face down on the desk. He sat, remembering the conversation with Coach O: "When you read their responses, look for a central theme or themes for each of the questions to the answers they gave."

"This is not about me," he whispered. "This is about them. I need to know how they feel." Slowly he turned the pages over.

Although none of them had signed the pages, he clearly recognized their handwriting. Sara's over-frilled loops and circles. Aaron's left-handed and angular slants.

Mary's smooth and professional cursive. But their words made his chest tighten and his eyes moist.

And Aaron's curt two-word answer to the first question made Peter want to sprint down the hall and hug his son.

What do you like that I do?
Not much.

Instead, he took a deep, steadying breath and focused on the central themes.

What do you like that I do?
Central theme from all the responses: When you spend special time with us, *uninterrupted.*

What do I need to stop doing immediately?
Central theme from all the responses:

Put your phone down at home and don't pick it up.

What do you want me to do more of or start doing?
Central theme from all the responses: Put us first and work second; spend more time with us.

As Peter looked over the simple answers he received from his family, he realized why Coach O had given him these specific questions. They forced his family to tell him the truth. Truth he needed to hear, and not just what he wanted to hear—or what they might think he wanted to hear. These truly were three truth-producing questions.

All right. He heard them. *But now what?*

He called Coach O, who seemed to be waiting on him. "You got the answers sooner than you expected, didn't you?"

"I did."

"They hurt?"

"More than you can imagine."

"No doubt. Just remember I've walked this path too, brother. Tell me what themes came out in their answers."

Peter read the response and the central themes he got from the answers. "What did you do next?"

"Peter, take things slowly. And I agree with your assessment. Remember you can also gain wisdom from your one-on-one meetings with your staff. If you listen well, they may teach and help you more than you help them."

Peter thought for a moment. Mark had also mentioned his problems at home—and a possible solution suggested by his pastor. "Coach, when I talked to Mark, he wanted to have time with his wife and kids individually. To set up what he called 'date nights.'"

"Sounds like a good idea, a new start for rebuilding his relationships. You think it would work with your family?"

"I think so. Definitely worth a try. I'll have one-on-ones with each of them, but since they are not exactly happy about my work right now . . . date nights sounds more friendly."

Coach laughed. "It does. When's your next family meeting?"

"Tomorrow night."

"Present it to them. And keep me posted."

Dinner that night was quiet, and the next day, Peter spent part of his Thursday putting together a family plan. He just hoped his family would embrace it as well.

That night, the scene looked all too familiar. The kids with their phones; Mary waiting patiently. Peter sat on the coffee table facing them.

"I want to open with prayer." He extended his hands, palms up.

They stared at him a moment, then exchanged looks. The phones went down and they leaned in, clasped hands forming a circle. Peter spoke softly.

"Lord, thank you for the blessings you have given this family. We are your children. Help us to remember that, to put you first in our lives. And right now, we are hurting.

Help us follow you and find a path that will heal us and bond us as a family. Amen."

They dropped hands, and this time they each watched Peter closely. He took a deep breath.

"I read your responses. I hear you. I truly hear what you're saying. I've been negligent and focused too much on what's outside, not what's inside.

Things are going to change, and I'll need your help. Habits are hard to break, and you may need to remind me."

"I can do that," muttered Sara.

Peter smiled. "I have no doubts about that." He looked at her, then Aaron, then Mary. "Here's my promise to each of you. This family will be first in my life, after the Lord. When I am home, the cell phone will not be my constant companion. If there's an emergency at work, I will give my team a different way to reach me. And I ask you to do the same. When we are together, put the phones down."

"But—"

Peter put up his hand. "Sara, let me finish, please." She hesitated, then nodded. He went on.

"I know our lives are busy, and I don't want to disrupt the schedules you already have in place. But I want us to eat together as much as possible. And I *will* be here. We will find time to do things together as a family, and we'll plan them out, so you can continue with other activities. And one night a month, I want to do something with each of you, just the two of us. I've lost track of what's important to you. That needs to change. So, I'm asking that you give up one night a month to spend with me. Do you think that's possible?"

Sara and Aaron looked at each other, then back at Peter. They both nodded.

"So that's your assignment for tonight. Pick a date. Pick what you want to do. This doesn't mean we won't do other things together. I'm still going to take Aaron to basketball camp. We'll still have meals out. But we need to spend time, just one-on-one. Are you up for it?"

Aaron nodded. Sara's mouth twisted, then her eyes widened in defiance. "We will if you will. You promise you'll change?"

Peter straightened. "I do." He turned to Mary. "Do you remember that drive-in theater?"

She grinned.

"They're playing *The Karate Kid* this weekend."

"The 1984 version or 2010?"

"1984."

"You're on."

Sara's mouth fell open. "You're going to take Mom to a drive-in movie?"

Peter stood up. "Yep. We might even make out in the back seat."

"Eww! TMI!"

Mary laughed and stood up next to Peter. "Get used to it, darlin'."

Peter pointed at Sara. "Bikes, Saturday morning?"

His daughter nodded, a smile peeking through. "OK."

Peter sat down next to Aaron. "I hear there's a new X-men comic coming out this week."

Aaron glanced up at him, then back at his hands. He nodded.

"Isn't Mac's Comic Emporium open on Sunday?"

Another hesitant nod.

"How about we go after church?"

A shrug, then . . . "OK. Thanks, Dad."

Peter almost shouted. Instead he pulled Aaron into a major bear hug. Aaron returned it briefly, then squirmed out of Peter's arms. "Just don't do that in public. OK?"

"Promise." Peter stood. "One more prayer." They all stood.

Sara took his hand tightly. "We're going to need lots of them."

"Amen," said Mary.

As he closed their family meeting in prayer, Peter felt a flush of hope.

They had a plan and a goal. And, with work, a solid future.

CHAPTER 8
The Journey Begins

It had been nearly a year since that difficult meeting with the board and the boardroom seemed as if it had not changed. It still smelled like furniture polish and coffee. Joe again sat to the left of the empty chair at the end of the table. The five men and four women of the board occupied the same chairs, tablets in front of them.

This time, however, Peter had a better idea of what was to come. He had prepared the answers he expected they would need, securely tucked into the presentation folders he carried.

Joe motioned for him to sit. "You know we're here to discuss the results of the latest employee surveys." Peter nodded, and Joe went on. "I have to admit, we're all a bit astonished. We expected the numbers to be up somewhat, but we didn't realize we'd see a likeability skyrocket."

"We've made some significant changes."

"Remarkable changes, apparently. We want to hear more about it. What in the world did you do?"

"Sir, it all started with a visit to a basketball camp." He passed out the folders, addressing the board at large. "And an encounter with a coach who had traveled the same journey five years ago. In these folders, you will find a copy of a newsletter, some general notes, and two 3 x 5 cards. These are the tools that led me to reconfigure how we conduct evaluations and reviews, how teams interact with each other, and the nature of changes I instituted in this company . . . even within my own family.

"The core of these changes is a series of one-on-one meetings geared toward building closer relationships with all employees and making people feel not only valued but wanted."

Peter opened the folder in front of him, and he led the board through an explanation of the documents inside. Their interest seemed to grow more intense as he spoke about his meetings with Coach O, Mark and his executive team, and his own family.

He brought the presentation to a close.

"**The bottom line is that the one-on-one meeting is, in fact, the most powerful, the 'greatest motivational tool' I have ever encountered in my 30-year career.**

It is an extremely potent motivator and relationship builder. When done correctly, it makes people feel cared about, heard and valued. My executive team has put this into place with their direct reports, and those teams have begun using it as well. The changes are cascading through the entire company, and our goal is to phase in this new process of one-on-one meetings for every department, and eventually with every team.

We want this structure to be a staple of our work environment and the primary force behind our *people first* culture."

Peter faced Joe again. "And I want to thank you—and the board. If you had not held my feet to the fire about the likeability scores, I would never have begun this journey. And I could have lost everything I hold dear."

Joe, who had been flipping through his folder spoke, "Well, we knew when we made you CEO that you could run a company. Now we know you can respond to a crisis and manage your people through it. I suspect you won't need to worry about your future here." He held out his hand, and Peter shook it. A great weight left his shoulders, and he stood up, thanking them all.

Peter headed back to his office, and Gabrielle met him with a tablet. "Your messages are on here, and I've also sent them to your phone. One is from Coach O. He just wants to check in. And I know it's a Friday afternoon, but at least two of the other messages are clients saying they needed to speak with you right away. That it's urgent. And Mary is in your office. Something about a date?"

Peter grinned. "Are those messages more urgent than a date with my wife?"

Gabrielle tilted her head to one side, her eyes narrowed in thought. "Hm. Honestly . . . probably not. The callers think they are, but . . ." She shook her head. "No, sir. They can wait."

"That's why you are so important to us here, Gabrielle. You can see through the . . . nonessentials. Thank you."

"I do my best."

He took the tablet and went into his office. Mary sat on the couch, reading her own tablet. Peter put everything on the desk and shut down his computer. "Are you ready?"

Mary slid the tablet into her bag and stood up. "As always. Where are we headed tonight?"

"That Italian place on East 24th."

She scoffed. "That little hole in the wall place?"

Peter stiffened in mock offense. "I'll have you know that 'hole in the wall' has the best stuffed manicotti and cannoli on the planet and I only take my favorite people there."

"Well, then, we'd better go before you change your mind."

Peter pulled her into a hug and kissed her gently. "Not going to happen."

They headed out, with a quick goodbye to Gabrielle. As they got into the Jeep, Peter asked, "How did yesterday go with Sara's ballet class?"

Mary fastened her seat belt. "Good, I think. But we're getting close to a decision."

"What's that?"

"Ballet or volleyball. I don't know if she can keep up both. Not with the high school activities picking up."

"So she's doing OK in school?"

"She wants to run for a student government office."

"Seriously?"

"You've inspired her."

"Me?"

Mary paused.

> **"Peter, I would never have thought the promises you made months ago, the changes you wanted, would have made such a difference.**

I know we have more to do, but Aaron has come out of his shell and Sara doesn't act like she has a future as a drama queen anymore."

"There's always next week."

They laughed, but Mary went on. "I'm sorry I doubted you."

"Don't be. I hadn't exactly engendered a lot of confidence with my behavior the last couple of years."

"True. But I knew the good man I married was still in there somewhere. Thank you for digging him out."

As the manicotti and cannoli settled, they took a walk in the neighborhood then returned home. Peter retreated briefly to his home office to return a missed call from Coach O. "What's up?"

"Nothing urgent. I want to follow up with you about the changes you've made. Can you meet for coffee Monday morning?"

"Sure. Same place, same time?"

"Sounds good."

CHAPTER 9
Unconditional Mentor

On Monday, Peter arrived a little early at the little coffee house. He bought a latte and settled in at a corner table near the back of the shop. He'd brought his notes from the first meeting, and an ever-expanding folder that held comments on other meetings. Coach O arrived a few moments later and greeted Peter with a firm handshake.

"Thanks for meeting me, Peter."

"Are you kidding? Thank *you.* I can't believe it's already been almost a year since that day at Aaron's basketball camp. It feels like a lifetime ago. I will be forever grateful that we saw each other that day."

Coach O nodded. "When you start this process, things can move quickly. So bring me up to date. How did the board meeting go?"

The words tumbled out in a rush of gratitude. Peter started with the board meeting and how not only his own employee engagement and likeability scores had gone up significantly but also those of his executive team. How instituting the one-on-one meeting structure had permeated through the company, making improvements on all levels. How Mark's home and work balance had settled, and how his own family had responded to "date nights."

"I would not have believed it. Mary and I are going out once a week, and I think our marriage has strengthened over the past months. I'm taking Sara and Aaron out once a month, and they are acting more like themselves again. Aaron even talks to me."

Coach clapped him on the shoulder. "Peter, that's fantastic! A serious blessing. You've taken the first steps, but there's so much more to do."

Peter frowned. "How do you mean?"

Coach leaned a little closer. "Let me start by asking this. How's the limitations on the cell phones working out?"

Peter took a deep breath and let it out slowly. "I admit that's been hard. For all of us. The kids haven't really known a life without a cell phone. I think Sara got her first one when she was six. Setting them aside for family time has been a struggle."

"I'm sure. Peter, one thing my coaching consultant impressed on me is that when you start making these changes, some great results will happen immediately.

But this isn't a quick fix or one-time event. It's a process. This is like marriage—you don't just want a great wedding, you want a great marriage.

It's going to be tough. The harder thing is to stay with it for the long run, to be completely committed to these changes. And it'll be extremely easy to fall back on your old ways: Relying on the phone. Shutting yourself off, isolating. Working longer than you have to. Trying to impress the wrong people. Chasing success rather than impact.

"So I want to encourage you to persevere. Don't fall away from the meetings. Make sure you keep them going. People are messy and relationships are fluid."

Peter nodded in agreement.

"In order to be sure these meetings don't turn into a checkbox on a report each month, you must view these as more than one-on-one meetings. You must see them as coaching and mentoring opportunities and you must see yourself as an unconditional mentor. This means you are willing to help anyone.

Your job as a leader is to help people move from knowledge to understanding and then to wisdom. You may be just coaching them now, but what you are teaching can help them for a lifetime.

People change, and so will your company. Climate and culture are constantly evolving. So you need to stay out in front of it. Keep meeting with your people; pour into them. The same with your family; be intentional. You need to keep doing this the rest of your life. But you can't do it alone."

Peter looked up, "I'll need help. Accountability."

"Exactly. You have to build your 'Mount Rushmore.' You need three or four people you trust, people who will really hold you accountable and encourage you. I will be one of yours."

Peter couldn't believe it. "Even more reason to be grateful. So, can I be one of yours?"

"You already are. 'As iron sharpens iron . . .'"

Peter knew the proverb by heart. " . . . so one person sharpens another."

"Truth. We both have a lot of work ahead of us, and together we can encourage each other. This is only the beginning of an ongoing process and change in your lifestyle.

Remember, the goal is to be fully engaged at work and fully engaged at home.

You want to control the pace of life, rather than having the pace of life control you."

Peter said, "Absolutely. And I have a new 'Why' for myself as I lead my family."

Coach O smiled. "Okay, big shooter. What is it?"

"When I'm traveling, it's my job to have my family miss me so much that they can't wait for me to come home, and when I'm home, I want them to never want me to leave."

"Good one, brother. We help those we lead get closer to their dreams every day. Welcome to the journey!"

Peter grinned. "A never-ending journey."

As Peter watched Coach O leave the coffee shop, he vowed to himself and God he would never turn back. He'd seen a glimpse of a remarkable future, one filled with hope and close relationships. That's where he truly belonged.

Epilogue

Mark arrived in Peter's office just after eight in the morning. He was a bit early for their standing 8:30 appointment, but Peter didn't mind. He and Mark had been meeting one-on-one for more than 11 months, and he'd watched the younger man grow exponentially in his leadership qualities and his relationships with his direct reports. Mark's likeability scores—as well as Peter's—had soared the last four quarters. The changes they had made in the ways they led their teams, along with being aware of their biases, had made remarkable improvements that echoed throughout the company.

Peter motioned for Mark to make himself a cup of coffee as he finished up a phone call. After he hung up, Peter poured another cup of coffee and joined Mark in the sitting area of his office. "My third so far," he said, motioning with the cup.

Mark smiled. "Fourth for me. I'll be jittery by noon if I don't stop."

"Getting enough rest?"

"Oh, yeah. Just want to stay sharp. I'm meeting with the department heads this morning for our one-on-ones."

"Perfect timing. That's one of the things I want to talk about this morning." Peter took a sip of coffee, then set the cup aside and leaned back in his chair. "It's been a little over four quarters since we implemented our changes, so I think it's time for us to have an overall update. The purpose of today's meeting is to address not just what you've done but the results of those changes. Let's start with the training program, and we'll finish up with a new type of OBT for you."

Mark straightened, the pride shining in his face as he went through the number of people who had eagerly signed on for the extensive training sessions he'd implemented, and how their individual, as well as their team, performances had improved. Productivity had increased 10 to 15 percent in most departments, and turnover had dropped significantly.

"People seem to have more satisfaction with what they do and achieve. And they've begun to encourage each other more. They've become more of a team and less siloed."

Peter nodded. "And your own scores have improved significantly as well. I'm proud of all you've accomplished."

"I wouldn't have believed it, no matter who said it, if you'd told me twelve months ago how the smallest changes could have the greatest impact.

I wouldn't have believed it." He paused, then plunged on. "Y'know, years ago, before my arrival here, I was trained that as a leader, no one was ever to say 'thank you' to people for just doing their job. You only got praised for going way beyond what was expected of you, and maybe not even then. I worked for a boss who absolutely expected all salaried employees to put in overtime, without either compensation or praise. It was a culture where we should just be grateful to have a job. But nothing could be more poisonous to morale."

"We just can't lead like that anymore."

"And I'm the walking, talking proof of that."

Peter laughed. "You've grown, that's for sure." He took another sip of coffee. "And I hear the rotating on-call schedule has smoothed out some coverage issues."

"Without a doubt. And thank you again for finding the money in the budget for a third shift manager."

"It helped with the work-life balance?"

"My wife, Beth, told me on a recent date night that it felt like we were on our honeymoon again. Just without the beach and room service."

"Good! Fighting for that balance can keep everything else in sync. It has for me."

Mark reached for the carafe of coffee, refreshed his cup, and asked Peter, "So things are better with your kids?"

"Took a bit of time—and a concentrated effort on mine and Mary's part—but yeah. Aaron's even talking to me again."

"Then there's hope for all of us with teenagers!"

"Absolutely."

They both fell silent a few moments, and Mark looked down at the coffee cup in his hand. He shifted in his chair and took a deep breath, but Peter beat him to the punch.

"That call I was on this morning when you came in?"

Mark scowled. "Yeah?"

"I suspect it wasn't supposed to happen until after this meeting."

The younger man froze, his eyes widening. "Ah."

"Mr. Samson is in a different time zone. He forgot. Probably out of his eagerness to talk to me."

"Peter, I'm sorry I—"

Peter put up a hand to stop Mark. "Let me finish." He took a deep breath as Mark looked miserable. "This is actually that 'different' OBT I wanted to talk to you about." At Mark's confused look, Peter leaned forward.

"Any leader worth their salt is going to want the people under him or her to grow. To improve. To stretch their wings. That's true leadership.

Anyone who wants people to remain stagnant and never progress or mature isn't much of a leader. Mark, you have at least 20 career years ahead of you. Did you think I'd expect you to stay my Chief Operations Officer that entire time?"

Mark looked relieved. "Not exactly. But I did want to tell you myself. I didn't want it to be a surprise."

"And you would have. But I'm thrilled that Samson is so eager to bring you on as their CEO. It's a tremendous opportunity. When did this all come about?"

"A few weeks ago. It happened because of our training and coaching program. Some of our trainers and coaches contract for Samson as well, and the network started buzzing when their current CEO resigned. They called me out of the blue."

"Because . . . when you're good, word gets out. What's your transition plan?"

"I want to work with you on it."

"Of course. What . . ."

"Two months to get someone in my place. A month of training. Starting with Samson after that."

"Sounds like a plan to me. Let your direct reports know, and we'll put together an email alerting the organization, and then we can put a team together to help ensure this all happens correctly." Peter stood and held out his hand. "Mark, I'm proud of you."

Mark shook his hand as he stood. "Not disappointed?"

"I'm always going to be disappointed to lose a good leader, but I would never want to hold one back."

Peter then moved from the handshake to giving Mark a firm hug and pat on the back. This time it was Peter's eyes that were beginning to moisten.

Peter escorted Mark out of his office, clapped him on the shoulder, and closed the door. He released a long breath. He *was* disappointed, but Mark's growth and potential for advancement couldn't be denied. And Peter *was* proud that the changes he had instituted had led to this.

Mark had a good team in place, and Peter's mind already buzzed with potential replacements. Time to train a new group of young people to grow and lead.

As he turned back toward his desk, he caught a glimpse of a picture reflecting in his office window. He moved over to his desk and picked up the framed picture of his family. His family life had come along way over the past twelve months too.

He and Mary had worked hard on their marriage. The counseling sessions had been surprisingly uplifting and productive. He had committed to dating his wife weekly and he now understood how important intentionality truly is. Like Coach O had said, it's one thing to have a great wedding, but now they wanted a great marriage.

His eyes moved to his kids, Aaron and Sara. Ever since that day in the park when Sara spoke hard truths to him, he'd been vigilant about placing a high priority on time with his children and on having a sniper focus whenever he was with them.

With children it's about quantity, not just quality.

His relationship with Sara was improving. Week by week trust was being rebuilt. There is nothing more special than a daddy's relationship with his daughter, and he was committed to staying the course. And he and Aaron had been spending time together consistently. Their impromptu pick-up basketball games in the driveway had been therapeutic for their relationship.

His phone buzzed. It was a text from Coach O... *time for coffee?*

APPENDIX

One-on-One Player Meeting Progression

1. Give them the three Ps of the meeting

2. Tell them two things you really like about them that you've seen in preseason workouts.

3. Tell them why you recruited them and how you've seen that come through so far (start communicating what their role is).

4. State the "One Big Thing" you want them to get better at before Game 1.

5. Have them restate numbers 3 & 4 back to you. Tell them you love 'em and glad they are playing for you.

One-on-One Executive Meeting Progression

1. Give them the three Ps of the meeting

2. Tell them why you hired them and how you've seen that come through so far (start communicating what their role is).

3. Ask them how they like working here on a scale of (1-10)
* Ask how you could help them raise the evaluation number?
3a. Ask them how their work/life balance is on a 1-10 scale?
* Ask how you could help them raise the evaluation number?

4. State the "One Big Thing" you want them to get better at this month or quarter.

5. Have them restate number 4 back to you.
* Tell them you Love 'em and are so glad they are working with you.

Acknowledgements

The Greatest Motivation Tool was birthed out of my work with college coaches and high-level executives and leaders. The processes described in this book are not theory; they are practical and being used by me and hundreds of successful leaders and coaches.

This book was birthed out of one of my e-newsletters I write monthly and by my friends. I want to thank Jon Gordon for encouraging me to write it, and I especially want to thank all the coaches and leaders I work with for their unending desire to learn and grow. You've impacted my life greatly and this book wouldn't exist if it weren't for your unceasing hunger for growth and connection.

Thank you to all the people who helped bring this book together and especially Ramona Richards. You are an angel sent from God. Also, a great amount of thanks to my many colleagues who have given me real-time input and advice for the fable and its contents.

Thank you to my children (who are now adults) for your encouragement and advice, and I especially want to thank Colt for his creativity in making all my stories complete.

I want to express my gratitude to my wife, Marla, who continues to put up with a 17-year-old boy in a 50-year-old man's body. You've changed my life and without your encouragement and support, I couldn't do what I do. Thank you and I love you more today than ever.

Finally, it may not be politically correct in today's world to write this, but if not for my faith in Jesus Christ and his death and resurrection, I would have nothing. Thank you, Lord.

About the Author

ROD OLSON, or "Coach O" is a catalyst and Coaches' coach known for his ability to help high-performing leaders find their "sweet spot" as they lead and motivate others in the 21st century. He is the founder of the Coaches of Excellence Institute and the Coach O Consulting Group.

Rod is also the highly regarded author of *The Legacy Builder* and *The Wisdom Lunch Warrior*. He is a nationally recognized speaker and leadership consultant specializing in coaching and culture development. Rod has clients in the corporate sector, professional and collegiate sports and our United States military special forces. Rod is a husband, father and coach. If you want more information on Rod, how to purchase his books or have him speak to your leaders, he can be reached at www.RodOlson.org. Follow **@CoachOTip** on Twitter for FREE Daily Tips from Coach O!

Get the original e-Newsletter that Coach O describes in *The Greatest Motivational Tool* plus more great information and resources from the author Rod Olson at:

RodOlson.org/Newsletter

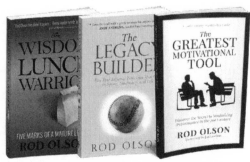

To purchase Rod's books, please visit:

RodOlson.org